STATE OF
EMERGENCY

PAIRED:

Two men who recorded stories about survivors of Hurricane Katrina. Josh Neufeld (left) illustrated the story of two friends who braved the worst of the storm. Dave Eggers wrote about the ordeal of a man who was just trying to help.

"Looking for adventure, Abbas and Darnell decided to stay behind to protect Abbas's store from looters. They thought they were prepared for anything. The two friends survived the storm. The next morning they celebrated, thinking the danger was past. Until the floodwaters started to rise. And rise."

Josh Neufeld

"[Zeitoun] felt restless, trapped.
The water was too deep to wade into, its
contents too suspect to swim through.
But there was the canoe. He saw it floating
above the yard, tethered to the house . . .
He imagined floating alone through the
streets of his city. In a way, this was a new
world, uncharted. He could be an explorer.
He could see things first."

Dave Eggers

Photographs © 2012: AP Images: 64 (Brett Coomer/Houston Chronicle), 18 (David J. Phillip),
back cover right, 3 (Katy Winn); FEMA News Photo/Jocelyn Augustino: 10, 60;
Getty Images: 16 (James Nielsen/AFP), 94 (David Portnoy), 76
(Corey Sipkin/NY Daily News), 82 (Mario Tama), 88 (Omar Torres/AFP);
Josh Neufeld: back cover left, 3 left (Photo by Seth Kushner), cover art;
NEWSCOM: 93 (Khampha Bouaphanh/KRT), 67 (Ammar Adb Rabbo);
Polaris Images: 70, 99 (Julie Dermansky), 100 (Riccardo Musacchio/Grazia Neri);
Random House, Inc.: 22, 24, 25, 26, 28, 29, 30, 32, 33, 34, 36, 37, 38, 40,
41, 42, 44, 45, 46, 48, 49, 50, 52, 53, 54, 57, 58 (Adapted from *A.D.:
New Orleans After The Deluge* by Josh Neufeld, copyright © 2009 by Josh Neufeld.
Used by permission of Pantheon Books, a division of Random House, Inc.);
Reuters: 74 (Vincent Laforet), 62, 86 (Rick Wilking); U.S. Navy
Photo/Photographer's Mate First Class Brien Aho: 79.

Library of Congress Cataloging-in-Publication Data

Wilson, Sari, 1968-
State of emergency / Sari Wilson.
p. cm. -- (On the record)
Includes bibliographical references and index.
ISBN-13: 978-0-531-22551-6
ISBN-10: 0-531-22551-8
1. Hurricane Katrina, 2005--Juvenile literature. 2. Disaster
relief--United States--Juvenile literature. 3. Rescue work--United
States--Juvenile literature. 4. Volunteers--United States--Juvenile
literature. 5. Neufeld, Josh. I. Title.
HV636 2005 .U6 W55 2012
976'.044--dc22

2011009419

Tod Olson, Series Editor
Marie O'Neill, Creative Director
Curriculum Concepts International, Production

11 12 13   40   21 20 19

STATE OF EMERGENCY

True tales of survival in the wake of Hurricane Katrina

Sari Wilson

Contents

Introduction:
Hurricane Katrina

Early on the morning of Monday, August 29, 2005, Hurricane Katrina hit land near New Orleans, Louisiana. Winds over 140 miles per hour ripped through towns and cities along the coastline of the Gulf of Mexico. The storm tossed stoves and refrigerators into the street and shredded them into bits of metal and plastic. Powerful gusts tore the roofs off houses. Torrential rains turned streams into rivers and lakes into sprawling swamps.

Along the Gulf Coast, Katrina created a giant wall of water known as a storm surge. The surge swamped coastal towns from Mobile, Alabama, to New Orleans. It knocked houses and huge buildings off their foundations. Streets and bridges were washed away. By one estimate, 90 percent of the buildings within a half-mile of Mississippi's coastline were destroyed.

Katrina plunged lives into chaos all along the coast. People left homeless by the storm swam for their lives, carrying pets in their arms. Others dragged sick or elderly relatives through the floodwaters on makeshift rafts. Stray dogs, abandoned or orphaned, wandered through the debris.

New Orleans was particularly vulnerable. About half of the city is below sea level and surrounded by water. Raised walls known as levees line the banks of lakes and rivers to keep the water out. City officials were afraid the storm surge would overwhelm the levees and cause massive flooding.

The morning before the storm, Mayor Ray Nagin had ordered the city's 450,000 residents to evacuate. More than three-quarters of the population piled into cars and buses and fled.

On Monday night, Katrina moved inland, away from New Orleans. Those who had stayed behind breathed a sigh of relief. But then disaster struck. Rising water overwhelmed the city's levees, one by one. Low-lying neighborhoods were covered in 20 feet of water. Only the rooftops of houses showed. By Tuesday evening, 80 percent of the city was under water.

Desperate survivors made their way to the city's giant sports stadium, the Superdome. By Wednesday, it held more than 20,000 people. Inside the sweltering stadium, conditions were brutal. The bathrooms overflowed with human waste. People slept on cardboard and covered themselves with vinyl ripped from the stadium walls. National Guard troops tried to keep order.

All around the city, residents climbed into attics and onto rooftops to escape the rising water. Local officials and ordinary citizens cruised the streets in boats trying to rescue survivors. Coast Guard helicopters airlifted families from their roofs.

Federal help was slow in coming. On Thursday, September 1, the U.S. government said that it would increase the number of National Guard troops in the city to 30,000. Meanwhile, rumors of violence spread throughout the city. The National Guard arrested hundreds of people and charged them with looting.

In the end, the cost of Hurricane Katrina was enormous. At least 1,800 people died from the storm and the flooding it caused. Billions of dollars' worth of property was destroyed. More than 350,000 evacuees were forced to move into temporary housing. Many would never return to their homes.

Shocked Americans wondered why the wealthiest country in the world hadn't been prepared to handle the disaster. The government formed committees to determine what had gone wrong. Many artists and writers also felt driven to understand what had happened—and to seek out the human stories behind the tragedy of Katrina.

PICTURING KATRINA

After Hurricane Katrina, cartoonist
Josh Neufeld volunteered to help survivors
on the ruined Gulf Coast. He met two men
whose story of survival and friendship
haunted him. He told their story in
a graphic book about the storm.

Six days after Hurricane Katrina struck New Orleans, two cars litter the rooftop of a home. The cars were swept onto the roof by floodwaters that rushed through the city after the levees collapsed.

1
Into the Storm

Josh Neufeld was 1,200 miles from New Orleans, in a small town in upstate New York, when Hurricane Katrina struck land. He had no TV and bad radio reception. He found pictures of the disaster in the newspaper and on the Internet. But that wasn't enough.

Neufeld, an illustrator and a cartoonist, wanted to witness the devastation himself. He wanted to understand what the survivors were going through. And he wanted to help.

As soon as Neufeld returned to his home in Brooklyn, New York, he went to the local Red Cross to volunteer. He signed up for a training course in disaster relief. And on October 12, he boarded a plane for Biloxi, Mississippi.

In Biloxi, Neufeld worked on an Emergency Response Vehicle (ERV) team. ERV workers drove from house to house, handing out water, ice, and hot food.

The force of the hurricane had left a staggering mess. Boats had been tossed into trees. Entire houses had been ripped from the earth, leaving only the foundations. "There were steps leading to nowhere," Neufeld remembers.

But what affected him most were the survivors' stories. The people he helped were eager to talk about their experiences during the storm.

At night, when Neufeld returned to the Red Cross base, he'd record the stories he'd heard during the day. After three weeks, he returned home, his mind filled with stories and images from the storm. When the editor of an online magazine invited him to create a web comic about Katrina, Neufeld jumped at the chance. A few months later, he was in New Orleans interviewing survivors.

Among the people Neufeld interviewed were two friends, Abbas and Darnell. Neufeld included their story and four others in a graphic work that eventually became a book—*A.D.: New Orleans After the Deluge.* Abbas and Darnell's story follows.

2
Abbas and Darnell

Abbas owned a small grocery store in the Uptown section of New Orleans. He had come to the United States from Iran during college. He settled in the city, married, and had two children.

Abbas's store was his livelihood. When he heard about Katrina, he decided to stay and protect his business. Besides, there was something exciting about an approaching storm. Abbas had stayed in the city for Hurricane Georges in 1998 and Hurricane Frances in 2004. But this was supposed to be the big one. Abbas was going to ride it out with his old buddy Darnell.

So, anyway, that's what I'm thinkin'. If I stay here at the store, I should be okay. Uptown is higher ground than my place in the 'burbs. Plus, this building's nice and sturdy.

3
Splitting Up

As the storm approached, Abbas's wife, Mabeeba, decided to take their kids and evacuate their home in Metairie, a suburb just outside New Orleans. The mayor had ordered everyone out of the city, and she didn't want to risk staying behind.

But Abbas was determined to stick it out. His store was in a solid, 14-foot-high building made of concrete and bricks. Even if the city flooded, Uptown was on high ground. He was convinced that he and Darnell would be fine.

4
Settled In

By midday on Sunday, Katrina's winds had reached 175 miles per hour. In the afternoon, the National Weather Service predicted that much of the Gulf Coast area would be "uninhabitable" for weeks. Electricity would fail, and half the homes in the region could be damaged. "Water shortages," the forecast read, "will make human suffering incredible by modern standards."

Still, Abbas and Darnell were in good spirits when they moved into the store.

And in here I've got...

"some flashlights..."

"my video camera..."

"bug spray..."

"and the Red Cross first aid kit Leila gave me."

And my cell phone charger is in the car.

Bro, we are all set. It's gonna be just like "Survivor"!

5
Katrina Strikes

Winds and rain from Hurricane Katrina struck New Orleans late on Sunday night. For hours, the storm raged through the city. Gusts up to 135 miles per hour battered the deserted streets. The storm wiped out power lines. Almost the entire city went dark.

Abbas and Darnell could only hope that the building would protect them from the worst of the storm.

Darnell, you hear that? Sounded like somethin' hit the roof.

Aw, 's prob'ly just a tree branch or somethin'. We can check it out tomorrow...

Yeah, you right. Anyway, I'm gonna try gettin' some shots of the storm from the doorway.

Mm-hmmm ⸮glomp⸮

VSSHHH

Monday, August 29, 3:49 p.m. Uptown.

Darnell, it's really over. No more rain... and the sky is clear!

Yah, Katrina! You ain't so bad!

Heh. C'mon, let's check the store for damage.

6

Calm After the Storm

By Monday afternoon, Katrina had blown off to the northeast of New Orleans.

Abbas tried to reach his wife and kids on his cell phone. He couldn't get through. But soon, he thought, they would come back to the city. He and Darnell would be greeted as heroes.

Except for the sign outside, the store had escaped without damage. Abbas and Darnell put steaks on the barbecue to celebrate. They were feeling good—until they heard a news report on the radio.

Folks, we have new information--

PROPERTY OF SAINTS XXL FOOTBALL

--about a possible levee breach in the 17th Street Canal. Right now details are sketchy. We'll be sure to update this story as it develops...

Sure, like a couple of hours ago, when they said the Central Business District was floodin'!

...however, police have confirmed isolated incidents of looting since the storm passed.

Oh, man, Abbas! Come look outside

7
The Flood

By Tuesday, the news was bleak. Levees had failed all across the city. Water from Lake Pontchartrain and the Mississippi River poured into New Orleans. Abbas's store was completely flooded.

Abbas and Darnell moved supplies onto the roof of the toolshed, where they figured they would spend the night.

On the news, reporters warned that looters and armed gangs were roving the city in boats. Darnell grabbed his bat, and he and Abbas ventured out to the street.

Thing is, it don't look like there is anyone else. Seems like we're the only ones left...

Oh man, Abbas -- your Mercedes!

Well, it ain't too bad right now. But if it gets in the electrical in the dashboard, then It's ruined...

≥sigh≤

8

Mission of Mercy

Abbas and Darnell woke up Wednesday morning on the roof of the toolshed. They were covered with mosquito bites.

The city was drowning. Engineers were working hard to plug the levees with sandbags and concrete. Garbage had begun to gather in the floodwater. Dead bodies floated through the streets.

Darnell had asthma, and he was having trouble breathing. Still, the two friends decided to distribute supplies from the store to people who were stranded in their homes.

9
Last Stand

That night, Abbas and Darnell climbed onto the roof of the shed and tried to sleep. Murky, foul-smelling water surrounded them. Abbas still hadn't been able to reach his family. The humidity and the pollution were making Darnell's asthma worse.

U.S. Coast Guard helicopters patrolled the sky, airlifting survivors from their roofs. News reports claimed that 80,000 people had been stranded in the city. Although he had trouble convincing Darnell, Abbas knew that it was time to end their adventure.

No, Abbas -- I told you already. I ain't leavin' -- ≥wheeze≤ --without you.

But, Darnell, why stick around? The store's totally flooded. For goodness' sake, there are rats runnin' around in trees!

SQUEAK

SQUEE

'Zackly! I could say the same thing to you. ≥wheeze≤

SQUEE

QUEE

Look, bro -- like I said, I'll go... ≥wheeze≤... when you do.

NEW ORLEANS SAINTS

10
The Aftermath

Josh Neufeld spent six months interviewing Abbas and the other people whose stories he would tell in *A.D.* Then he spent three years drawing the comics. As the book took shape, he decided to find out what happened to his subjects after the storm.

Abbas and Darnell were among the lucky ones. They escaped from the destroyed city and began to rebuild their lives.

It took 16 months for Abbas to rebuild his store. Insurance paid for some of the work, but he had to take out a loan for the rest.

Darnell left New Orleans for good after the storm. His home had been completely destroyed and he didn't want to start from scratch. He moved to Atlanta, Georgia, and stayed with family there until he had the money to get his own place.

In 2008, Abbas finally reopened his store. He felt like he'd lost three years of his life. But at least his family was safe and he was back in business.

That, says Josh Neufeld, is the hopeful side to the stories that emerged from the devastation of Hurricane Katrina. "At the heart of *A.D.*," he says, "is that the lives of real people continue and the life of the city continues."

"What made you finally decide to get out of the flooded city?"

≡Wheeze≡

"To tell you the truth, Darnell's health. His asthma was gettin' real bad. He kept sayin' he wouldn't leave without me, so I just figured it was up to me."

"Some friends came by in a small boat. I grabbed the store's cash box and we got out."

"When we left, I couldn't even see my Mercedes anymore. The water was that deep."

MEALS
HOT MEALS

"Me and the family, we got back home the Tuesday following the hurricane."

"Once the water was gone, I went back to the store. I had left behind some important stuff--documents, family photos, things like that."

CALHOU
SUPERETT

"Anyway, the store was real bad. Disgusting, with the rotted meat, vegetables, and so on. I cleaned it myself."

Josh Neufeld's graphic novel *A.D.: New Orleans After the Deluge* (2009) received extensive press coverage and became a *New York Times* best seller.

Josh Neufeld

Born:

August 9, 1967

Grew up:

San Diego and San Francisco, California; and
New York City, New York

Day job:

Comic book artist and illustrator

Website:

www.joshcomix.com

Favorite books:

Safe Area Gorazde, Joe Sacco
Persepolis, Marjane Satrapi
Paul Auster's City of Glass, David Mazzucchelli
    and Paul Karasik
Tintin in Tibet, Hergé

Author of:

A.D.: New Orleans After the Deluge
*A Few Perfect Hours and Other Stories from
    Southeast Asia and Central Europe*
The Influencing Machine
Titans of Finance
The Vagabonds

He says:

"It's real stories that interest me most, and
I try to use the comics form to explore
'unconventional' subjects. I try in my drawings
to treasure the strangeness of real life and
appreciate the little details of daily existence."

BEARING WITNESS

Abdulrahman Zeitoun survived Hurricane Katrina only to be swept up by another powerful force: his own government. Then he met writer Dave Eggers, who wanted to tell his story to the world.

Two days after the hurricane hit New Orleans, a police car lies submerged in the flooded city. With the flood came lawlessness, as people did what they could to survive.

11

Witnessing Katrina

When Hurricane Katrina tore through New Orleans, it destroyed more than buildings and bridges. It crippled the city's government—including the entire justice system. Some 350,000 people evacuated in the days before the storm. With them went the city's judges, public defenders, court clerks, and prison guards. After the hurricane passed, at least 200 city police officers did not show up for work. All the jails in the area were underwater and absolutely useless.

On September 2, 2005, Louisiana State Police officers drive past residents stranded near the Convention Center in New Orleans. As many as 20,000 people may have taken refuge at the center in the aftermath of the storm.

In news reports, New Orleans looked and sounded like a lawless mess. TV coverage showed desperate people raiding grocery stores for diapers, food, and water. The cable network MSNBC even caught police officers looting clothes from a Wal-Mart store. Gunfights allegedly broke out around the city.

Into the chaos stepped the National Guard. Within a week, more than 30,000 National Guard troops had arrived in the city. Some worked hard to rescue people trapped by the flooding. The rest patrolled the streets, heavily armed and determined to restore order.

On Monday, September 5, a week after the storm, a makeshift jail opened in a Greyhound bus station. Before long, it was filled with prisoners. Most of them had been accused of looting. They were imprisoned in temporary pens topped with razor wire. No courts were functioning, so the prisoners weren't charged with crimes. Most were not allowed to make phone calls to let friends and family know where they were.

Like most Americans, writer Dave Eggers followed the disaster in the news. He was dismayed by what he saw. "There was a complete suspension of all legal processes. There were no hearings, no courts for months and months," he told a reporter from the website Salon.com.

Eggers felt that this part of the story had to be told. And he was in a position to tell it. In 2000, Eggers published a memoir called *A Heartbreaking Work of Staggering Genius.* It told the story of his

The Greyhound bus station in New Orleans was transformed into a prison camp. Many of the people detained there were later found innocent of any crimes.

parents' deaths when he was 21 and the years he spent raising his younger brother, Toph. The book became a best seller.

With his newfound fame—and money—Eggers started a tutoring center for kids at 826 Valencia Street in San Francisco, California. The idea caught on, and "826" centers were opened in seven other cities.

Along with human rights scholar Dr. Lola Vollen, Eggers also founded a project called Voice of Witness. It collects and publishes the stories of people who've been harmed by human rights abuses.

A few weeks after Katrina, Vollen and Eggers sent a Voice of Witness team to the Gulf Coast to interview Katrina survivors. In 2006, 13 of the stories were published in the book *Voices from the Storm*.

One of the narrators in the book was a Syrian American business owner named Abdulrahman Zeitoun. Zeitoun had stayed in the city to watch over his home and business. When the flood came, he paddled the streets in a canoe, bringing supplies to people in need. He was a one-man rescue crew—until the police abruptly put an end to his mission.

Eggers was haunted by the story. In 2006 he went to visit Abdulrahman Zeitoun and his wife, Kathy Zeitoun, in New Orleans. "In the first hour," Eggers told a British reporter, "it was clear there was so much to say." Three years later, he told the story in a book titled simply *Zeitoun*.

Abdulrahman Zeitoun stayed in New Orleans after Katrina, helping stranded people and dogs. When his brother urged him to flee the city, Zeitoun responded simply: "They need me here more. This is my family too."

12

Weathering the Storm

Zeitoun had lived in the United States for more than a decade when Katrina hit. New Orleans was his home, and he was well liked around the city. He and Kathy were raising four children and running a painting contractor's business. The Zeitouns also owned six buildings with a total of 18 tenants. People knew the company by its rainbow logo, which appeared on lawn signs, scaffolding, and the side of Zeitoun's van.

Both Zeitoun and Kathy were practicing Muslims. Kathy had been born in the U.S.

and raised a Baptist. She converted to Islam when she was in her early 20s. Zeitoun was raised in the Islamic faith in Syria.

On occasion, Zeitoun's Middle Eastern origins were enough to turn potential clients away. People would call for an estimate on a painting job and ask the origin of the name Zeitoun. When Kathy told them, they would say "never mind" and hang up. "It was rare," Eggers writes, "but not rare enough."

Two days before the storm, Kathy Zeitoun prepared to evacuate the city with their daughters. She made plans to stay with relatives in Baton Rouge, Louisiana. She begged her husband to come along.

But Zeitoun shook his head. His customers needed him, he said. And if he left, who would look after their house and business?

On August 29, while Kathy got settled in Baton Rouge, Zeitoun battled the storm. Their house creaked and moaned in the wind. Zeitoun stuffed pillows in blown-out windows. He put buckets under leaks and emptied them every hour.

The next morning, Zeitoun went to the window and saw a river of water gushing down the street. He slowly realized what had happened. The levees that held back Lake Pontchartrain had broken. The water was rushing in, flooding the city.

Zeitoun spent the day carting his family's possessions upstairs to safety. He took the TV and DVD player, books and games, everything he could carry. He watched as the lake water poured into his home. It swamped the phone box and the electrical box. He called Kathy on his cell phone.

Floodwaters from Lake Pontchartrain (foreground)
overwhelm levee walls. As the levees crumble,
lake water surges into New Orleans (background).

She begged him again to come to Baton Rouge. He gently refused and then went to sleep on the roof.

When he woke the next morning, he saw his secondhand canoe floating in the floodwaters, tied to the house. He had bought it on a whim several years back and had only used it a few times. Now he felt inspired. "He imagined floating alone through the streets of his city," Eggers writes. "In a way, this was a new world, uncharted. He could be an explorer. He could see things first."

Three men paddle boats down a flooded street in their neighborhood in New Orleans. One man is using a shovel as an oar.

13

Rescue Mission

On the morning of Wednesday, August 31, Zeitoun climbed into his canoe and navigated the streets. He picked up Frank Noland, a neighbor who wanted to check on his truck. As they paddled, they heard cries for help.

In one house, they found an 80-year-old woman trapped in her flooded living room. Her head was just inches from the ceiling. She was too big to fit in the canoe, so the two men left to find help.

They tried to wave down several motor-boats carrying uniformed soldiers or police. The boats simply swerved around the canoe, leaving it to sway in their wake. Zeitoun couldn't understand why the authorities ignored them. "Where were these boats going, what were they looking for, if not for residents of the city asking for help?" Eggers writes.

Finally, Zeitoun and Noland found a pair of fishermen in a motorboat who were willing to help. The fishermen towed Zeitoun and Noland back to the stranded woman. Then the men used a ladder to hoist her into the boat.

From there, the tiny rescue party continued on, picking up survivors along the way. Within a few hours, the fishing boat

A U.S. Coast Guard airboat patrols the flooded streets of New Orleans. The Coast Guard took part in Joint Task Force Katrina, a rescue mission that also involved the U.S. Army, Marines, and Air Force.

was full of elderly people. The fishermen would take the survivors to higher ground, where they could be evacuated.

Zeitoun and Noland said good-bye to the fishermen and paddled off. They felt good about their day's work.

Later that day, Zeitoun went to Claiborne Avenue to check on one of his rental properties. A tenant named Todd Gambino welcomed him, surprised to learn that Zeitoun had stayed in the city. Gambino had spent the day dragging his belongings to safety on the second floor. The house was full of mud, but the damage could have been worse.

Zeitoun found a working phone line at the house and called Kathy. She thanked God that he was alive. And she told him about the terrible reports she had been hearing on TV. The floodwater was polluted. Diseases were spreading. Looters were taking over the city.

"So when do you plan to leave?" she asked.

"I don't," he said.

Zeitoun promised to call each day at noon. He went home to spend another night on the roof.

A man and his son evacuate with their dogs. Many victims of the storm were forced to leave their pets behind.

14

Chaos

Every day for the next week, Zeitoun explored the ruined city. He paddled his canoe through the streets, looking for people to rescue. He checked on his properties. He fed abandoned dogs. At noon he would go to the house on Claiborne and call Kathy. Every day, she tried to convince him to leave. Every day, he refused. "He came to think that he had been put by God in the city for a reason," Eggers explained in a radio interview. "That that was his destiny—to be there after the storm and make himself useful."

Zeitoun wasn't alone in his rescue efforts. Coast Guard pilots pulled people off their roofs by helicopter. Officials from the Louisiana Fish and Wildlife Service rescued 3,000 survivors in the first two days after the storm. Ordinary citizens put their personal boats to use as rescue vehicles.

But after a day or two, the mood in the city grew tense. Airlift rescue operations were suspended when people reportedly shot at helicopters. Fires broke out near the Superdome and the Convention Center, where a total of 40,000 people had taken refuge. Reports of uncontrolled looting spread quickly in the media.

On September 2, Governor Kathleen Blanco announced that the National Guard had arrived, armed with rifles. "They have M16s and are locked and loaded," she warned. "These troops know how to shoot and kill and I expect they will."

New Orleans began to resemble a military zone. Soldiers patrolled the streets. On September 4, police officers shot at six unarmed men who were looking for food. Two of the men died and the other four were wounded.

Hundreds of people were arrested for looting—some of whom were taking only what they needed to survive. In one case, police arrested a 73-year-old grandmother for stealing sausage that she claimed was from the trunk of her own car.

This was the mood in New Orleans when Zeitoun pulled up to the Claiborne house on September 6. With him was a Syrian friend referred to as Nasser in *Zeitoun*.

A SWAT team armed with machine guns patrols downtown New Orleans.

Zeitoun took a shower and called his brother Ahmad, who lived in Spain. Just like Kathy, Ahmad warned him about the reports on TV. Armed gangs were taking over New Orleans, Ahmad said. Zeitoun shrugged it off. He hadn't seen anything like that in the week since the hurricane.

As he was getting off the phone, Zeitoun heard noises outside. When he looked up he saw six guards in military vests burst into the house.

Zeitoun told the soldiers that he owned the house; he was not a thief. It didn't seem to matter. The soldiers rounded up Zeitoun, Gambino, Nasser, and another survivor who had stopped by to use the phone. With no explanation, they shoved the prisoners into a military boat and took off.

Zeitoun was sent to "Camp Greyhound," a bus station that had been converted into a jail. The temporary facility held 1,200 detainees in the aftermath of Katrina.

15
Locked Up

Several hours after their arrest, Zeitoun and the others were taken to a Greyhound bus station, which had just reopened as a prison. Their hands had been bound behind them with plastic ties. Inside the station, about 80 uniformed men and women stood guard. Some of them held assault rifles. Two patrolled the room with guard dogs.

The soldiers questioned Zeitoun and the others. They strip-searched and photographed Zeitoun. Then they led the four men behind the station and threw them into open-air cages. Gambino had been given a reason for their arrest: looting. But when the prisoners begged to use a phone, they got a different explanation. "You guys are terrorists," a guard said.

Now they were in trouble, Zeitoun thought. Both Nasser and Gambino had been carrying large amounts of cash. Zeitoun and Nasser had Middle Eastern names. Since the terrorist attacks of September 11, 2001, the U.S. government had been keeping a close eye on people from largely Muslim countries. Zeitoun had never been hassled before. But he and Kathy had plenty of Muslim friends who had been investigated. Now he had come under suspicion, and he had no way to contact his wife or a lawyer.

Three days later, Zeitoun and the other men were bused to Hunt Correctional Center, 40 miles north of New Orleans. Zeitoun and Nasser ended up in the high-security wing of the prison.

After a few days, more prisoners arrived with stories similar to Zeitoun's. One man was a sanitation worker from Houston who had been sent to New Orleans to clear flood debris from the streets. He said he had been arrested while walking from his hotel to his truck. Another man had been moving furniture in his house when soldiers broke in and arrested him.

By now, New Orleans was dominated by law enforcement officials. The U.S. Army's 82nd Airborne Division evacuated the Superdome and the Convention Center. Other cities sent police officers to help keep order. By September 8, the main levees had been repaired, and the floodwater had been pumped out of the city. Looting was no longer a problem. But the city still looked like an armed camp.

Zeitoun, meanwhile, tormented himself in his cell. Why hadn't he listened to Kathy and left the city? He fell ill and despaired at the thought that he might die in prison. He prayed for a messenger, someone to tell Kathy he was alive.

On September 18, he got a visit from a Christian missionary. Zeitoun pleaded with the man to take Kathy's phone number and call her. "Zeitoun struggled to sleep that night," Eggers writes. "There was a man in the world who knew that he was alive. He had found his messenger."

Hundreds of people line up to be evacuated from New Orleans. The chaos in the aftermath of Katrina "exposed serious problems in our response capability at all levels of government," said President George W. Bush.

After Katrina, thousands of people were separated from their family members. Survivors often didn't know whether their loved ones had died, evacuated, or been hospitalized or imprisoned. Here, a woman looks at a message board set up to help reunite separated families.

16
Recovery

On September 19, Kathy got a call from Zeitoun's "messenger." For the first time in two weeks, she knew her husband was alive.

Later that day, a government official called Kathy to say that they were "not interested" in Zeitoun anymore. He would be released soon.

In reality, freeing Zeitoun would be much harder than the official suggested. It took Kathy two weeks, a lawyer, and a $10,000 bond to get her husband released.

Finally, a month after the hurricane, Kathy met Zeitoun in front of Hunt Correctional Facility. The couple cried and hugged. Zeitoun had lost 22 pounds. It would take him months to recover his health and energy. But he was alive, and back with his family.

In some ways, Zeitoun was fortunate. The three other men Zeitoun was arrested with spent five, six, and eight months in prison. Eventually the charges against all of them were dropped.

Eggers is angry about what happened to Zeitoun and his fellow prisoners. But he acknowledges that many of the law enforcement people did "phenomenal work" rescuing hurricane survivors. If some soldiers overreacted, he says, he can understand why. Many of them had been fighting in Afghanistan or Iraq. They had heard media reports of chaos in New Orleans. "Those that I talked to," Eggers said on National Public Radio, "really felt they were entering a war zone."

Instead of placing blame, Eggers set up a charitable foundation with the profits from *Zeitoun*. The foundation funds rebuilding projects in New Orleans and promotes human rights in the United States.

Since the book came out, Zeitoun has been called a hero in the media for his role in the Katrina rescue effort. "I really don't feel like we deserve all this attention," he told one reporter. "I only did what I had been brought up to do."

Zeitoun and Kathy returned to their home in New Orleans. They rebuilt their business and then got to work rebuilding the city. Zeitoun Painting and Contracting has restored schools, a museum, and more than 250 damaged houses.

Despite his ordeal, Zeitoun is optimistic about his adopted homeland. He refuses to consider leaving New Orleans. "This is my home, my city," he says. "My life is here now."

He even plans to buy a bigger boat. That way, when the next big hurricane arrives, he can rescue people more easily.

Abdulrahman Zeitoun, his wife, Kathy, and their four children pose for a photo nearly five years after Hurricane Katrina.

Dave Eggers wrote the book *Zeitoun* about Abdulrahman Zeitoun's ordeal after Hurricane Katrina. Eggers has donated all the money from the book sales to the Zeitoun Foundation, which works to rebuild New Orleans.

Dave Eggers

Born:

March 12, 1970

Grew up:

Chicago, Illinois

Life's work:

Writer, editor, publisher, and advocate for social justice. Eggers is the founder of McSweeney's, an independent publishing house in San Francisco.

Website:

www.zeitounfoundation.org

Author of:

A Heartbreaking Work of Staggering Genius (memoir)
How We Are Hungry (short stories)
You Shall Know Our Velocity! (novel)
What Is the What (novel)
The Wild Things (novel)
Zeitoun (nonfiction)

He says:

"Writing is a deep-sea dive. You need hours just to get into it: down, down, down. If you're called back to the surface every couple of minutes by an email, you can't ever get back down."

A Conversation with Author
Sari Wilson

Q *How did you conduct your research for the book?*

A First I read *A.D.* and *Zeitoun* closely and thought about what made them similar and what made them different. I also read tons of books and newspaper and magazine articles on the hurricane and its aftermath. I got so I could tell you the day and hour Katrina struck, and the whole timeline of what happened. I knew what Abbas and Zeitoun were doing almost every hour of those early days.

Q *Did you speak personally with Neufeld or Eggers?*

A I did speak to Neufeld—because he is my husband! We both work at home, so I went into the other room, which is his studio, and interviewed him. I actually got to know a different side of him while writing this book.

I didn't get to speak personally to Eggers because he was traveling and out of the country. But I spoke with a bunch of people who were associated with Voice of Witness and his other ventures. That was really helpful.

Q *What did you learn about Hurricane Katrina that surprised you?*

A Part of the reason that Katrina hit New Orleans so hard is that the wetlands that surround the Gulf and New Orleans are disappearing. So even though there have been really big storms and powerful hurricanes in the past, now there is less of a buffer—less padding—to protect the Gulf Coast during storms.

Q *Do you think it was irresponsible for Zeitoun, Abbas, and Darnell to stay behind when people had been ordered to evacuate New Orleans?*

A Yes, but that is what makes these stories so real. We've all done things that we shouldn't do because we thought we were doing something important. Both Zeitoun and Abbas thought they serving a higher purpose—Zeitoun wanted to protect his house and help survivors and Abbas wanted to protect his store. They also shared an eagerness for adventure. Those things seem really human to me.

Q *What do you think drove Abbas and Zeitoun to return to New Orleans after Katrina?*

A I think they felt a loyalty to their city. I live in New York City, and I felt a similar way after the terrorist attacks on the World Trade Center on 9/11. The whole city pulled together and people became weirdly nice to each other. I think disasters often make people feel more connected to each other and to the place where they occur.

Q *Why do you think the justice system failed Zeitoun?*

A After 9/11, the federal government made a huge effort to hunt down terrorists. FEMA [the agency in charge of disaster relief] had been placed under the Homeland Security Agency. All of the funding for Homeland Security was going to anti-terrorism work, and the agency wasn't able to see beyond that mission. Even in a human catastrophe like Katrina, they saw threat and danger from many lost and desperate people who simply needed help. It doesn't mean that there weren't a lot of brave and devoted law officers and public officials. But there was something wrong with the system at the time.

Q *How did Josh Neufeld get into cartooning?*

A Josh has been drawing comics since he was four! In his first apartment, he had a tiny bedroom. His bed was on a loft so that he could have room for his drawing table. When I first met him, he was drawing superhero comics. Soon after we met, he realized that he wanted to draw comics about real life.

Q *Why did Neufeld and Eggers feel compelled to engage others and tell the stories of Katrina?*

A They both felt compelled to tell these stories because of their own passions. Josh volunteered in the Gulf Coast after Katrina because he wanted to help people. He was really moved by the stories he heard from survivors. When he came back, it was all he talked about. He began to write about those stories so he could engage with a wider audience. Eggers is moved to tell the stories of people who have suffered injustice. When he saw what was happening in New Orleans and heard Zeitoun's story, he wanted to do something about human rights violations. So he wrote about Zeitoun's experience to engage others in that story.

What to Read Next

Fiction

Does My Head Look Big in This?, Randa Abdel-Fattah. (368 pages) *This funny novel tells the story of an Australian Palestinian girl who is a devout Muslim and a typical teenager.*

Hurricane Song, Paul Volponi. (144 pages) *Sixteen-year-old Miles leaves his mother's home in Chicago and goes to stay with his father in New Orleans just before Hurricane Katrina.*

The Complete Maus: A Survivor's Tale, Art Spiegelman. (296 pages) *This graphic novel tells the story of a survivor of the Holocaust.*

Love, Ocean, Celia Anderson. (138 pages) *Ocean, a teenage girl who has survived Hurricane Katrina, faces life in a new town while her father is fighting in Iraq.*

Nonfiction

Arab in America, Toufic El Rassi. (117 pages) *This autobiographical graphic novel tells the story of Toufic, who moved to the U.S. from Lebanon when he was one year old.*

Daily Life of Arab Americans in the 21st Century, edited by Anan Ameri and Holly Arida. (272 pages) *About 3.5 million Arab Americans live in the United States. This book examines various aspects of the Arab American experience.*

Hurricane Force: In the Path of America's Deadliest Storms, Joseph P. Treaster. (128 pages) *This book is a history— with maps, diagrams, and photographs—of hurricanes in the U.S.*

Hurricane Katrina: Aftermath of Disaster (Snapshots in History), Barb Palser. (96 pages) *This book gives an overview of Hurricane Katrina and chronologically follows the storm's arrival, effects, and aftermath.*

Books

Voices from the Storm: The People of New Orleans on Hurricane Katrina and Its Aftermath, edited by Lola Vollen and Chris Ying. (250 pages) *This book presents real stories from real people who lived through Hurricane Katrina at ground level.*

Zeitoun, Dave Eggers. (368 pages) *This is Dave Eggers's book about what happened to Abdulrahman Zeitoun after Hurricane Katrina hit New Orleans.*

Tornadoes, Hurricanes, and Tsunamis: A Practical Survival Guide, April Isaacs. (64 pages) *This concise book gives facts about extreme weather conditions and valuable information about how to act during these events.*

Films and Videos

American Experience: New Orleans (2007) *This two-hour PBS documentary explores the history—and captures the unique culture—of New Orleans.*

National Geographic—Inside Hurricane Katrina (2005) *This film provides a clear picture of the elements, both natural and human-made, that contributed to the disaster in New Orleans.*

Websites

video.nationalgeographic.com/video/player/ environment/environment-natural-disasters/ hurricanes/html
This National Geographic site has amazing videos of hurricanes in action, including Katrina.

www.katrinadestruction.com
The photographs in this huge collection of Hurricane Katrina images are for sale, but you can view any or all of them for free.

Glossary

assault rifle (uh-SAWLT RYE-fuhl) *noun* a rifle with a detachable magazine that can fire single rounds or bursts of automatic fire

Baptist (BAP-tist) *noun* a member of various evangelical Protestant Christian sects who believe in being baptized after they publicly announce their beliefs

bond (BOND) *noun* a guarantee of money in exchange for releasing a prisoner until his or her trial

Coast Guard (KOHST GARD) *noun* the branch of the armed forces that watches the sea for ships in danger and protects the coastline

deluge (DEL-yooj) *noun* a heavy rain or flood

Gulf Coast (GUHLF KOHST) *noun* the shore around the Gulf of Mexico; in the United States it includes the coastlines of Texas, Louisiana, Mississippi, Alabama, and the west coast of Florida

human rights (HYOO-muhn RITEZ) *noun* the rights and freedoms that all humans are entitled to; including equality, justice, freedom of religion, and human dignity

Islam (i-SLAHM) *noun* the religion based on the teachings of the Koran, a book that Muslims accept as the word of Allah as told to the prophet Muhammad

levee (LEV-ee) *noun* a bank built alongside the waters of a river or lake to prevent flooding

loot (LOOT) *verb* to steal from stores or houses, often during a riot or a war

M16 (EM siks-TEEN) *noun* the primary assault rifle of the U.S. military since 1967

Muslim (MUHZ-luhm) *noun* someone who follows the religion of Islam

National Guard (NASH-uh-nuhl GARD) *noun* a volunteer military organization with units in each state in the U.S. Each unit is under the control of the state governor.

submerge (suhb-MURJ) *verb* to cover with water or another liquid

SWAT team (SWAHT TEEM) *noun* a heavily armed police unit trained to handle unusually dangerous or violent situations. *SWAT* is an acronym for "special weapons and tactics."

vulnerable (VUHL-nur-uh-buhl) *adjective* in a weak position and likely to be hurt or damaged in some way

whim (WIM) *noun* a sudden idea or wish

Metric Conversions

miles to kilometers: 1 mi is about 1.6 km

feet to meters: 1 ft is about 0.3 m

inches to centimeters: 1 in is about 2.54 cm

pounds to kilograms: 1 lb is about 0.45 kg

Sources

INTRODUCTION

CNN Reports: Katrina—State of Emergency, CNN News. Kansas City: Andrews McNeel Publishing, 2005.

The Great Deluge: Hurricane Katrina, New Orleans, and the Mississippi Gulf Coast, Douglas Brinkley. New York: HarperCollins, 2006.

"Hurricane History," National Hurricane Center. www.nhc.noaa.gov

"Hurricane Katrina." National Oceanic and Atmospheric Administration, December 29, 2005.

Hurricane Katrina: Devastation on the Gulf Coast, Debra A. Miller. Farmington Hills, MI: Thomson Gale, 2006.

Hurricane Katrina (Great Historic Disasters), Jamie Pietras. New York Infobase Publishing, 2006.

"Hurricane Katrina Timeline." *CBC News Online,* September 4, 2005.

"'This Is Our Tsunami.'" *Fox News,* August 30, 2005.

PICTURING KATRINA

Author's interview with Josh Neufeld in 2010. (including quotes on pages 4, 20, 56, 59)

A.D.: New Orleans After the Deluge, Josh Neufeld. New York: Random House, 2009.

"A Day with the Red Cross," Josh Neufeld. September 10, 2005.

Katrina Came Calling, Josh Neufeld. Josh Neufeld Comix and Stories, 2006.

"Katrina: Forecasting the Nation's Most Destructive Storm." National Oceanic and Atmospheric Administration, May 30, 2007. (including quote on page 31)

BEARING WITNESS

Zeitoun, Dave Eggers. San Francisco: McSweeney's Books, 2009. (including quotes on pages 5, 70, 72, 75, 78, 81, 90, 92, 97, 99)

"The Amazing True Story of Zeitoun," Ed Pilkington. *Guardian*, March 12, 2010. (including quotes on page 97, 98)

"Bush Takes Responsibility for Failures in Storm Response," Kirk Johnson and Christine Hauser. *New York Times*, September 13, 2005. (including quote on page 93)

"Dave Eggers' Heartbreaking Work of Staggering Reality," Andrew O'Hehir. Salon.com, July 16, 2009. (including quote on page 66)

"Ex-Cop Exposes Cover Up of Katrina Killings," Casey Gane-McCalla. NewsOne.com, February 25, 2010.

"'It Was as if All of Us Were Already Pronounced Dead'; Convention Center Left a Five-Day Legacy of Chaos and Violence," Wil Haygood and Ann Scott Tyson. *Washington Post*, September 15, 2005.

"A Man on a Mission," Rachel Cooke. *Observer*, March 7, 2010. (including quotes on pages 69, 101)

"New Orleans Begins Confiscating Firearms as Water Recedes," Alex Berenson and Timothy Williams. *New York Times*, September 8, 2005. (including quote on pages 84–85)

"Q&A: Author Dave Eggers," Claire Suddath. *Time*, July 22, 2009.

Voices from the Storm: The People of New Orleans on Hurricane Katrina and Its Aftermath, Lola Vollen and Chris Ying. San Francisco: McSweeney's Books, 2006.

"War on Terror, Katrina Intersect in *Zeitoun*." NPR's *All Things Considered*, July 25, 2009. (including quotes on pages 83, 97)

Index